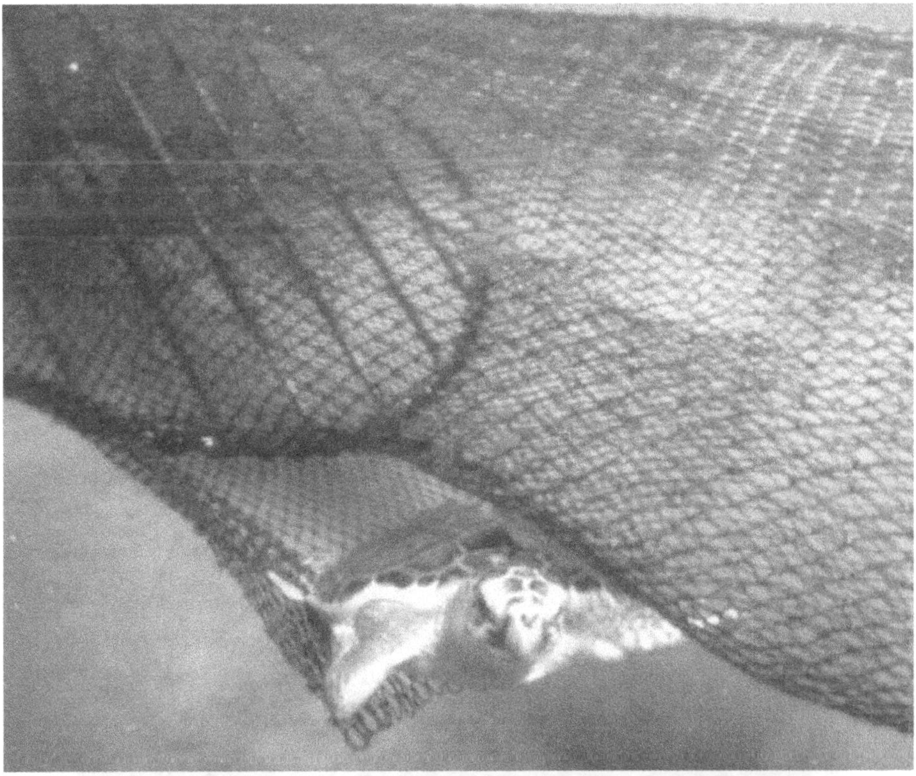

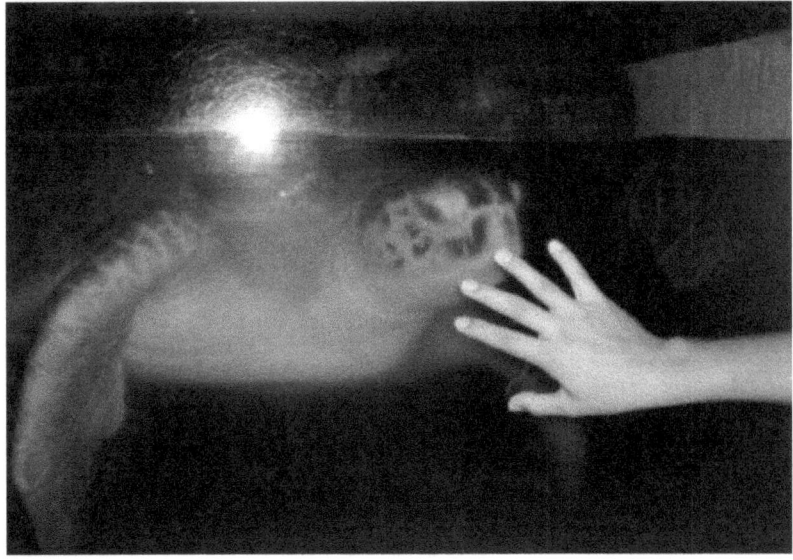

Cute Turtle Pets...

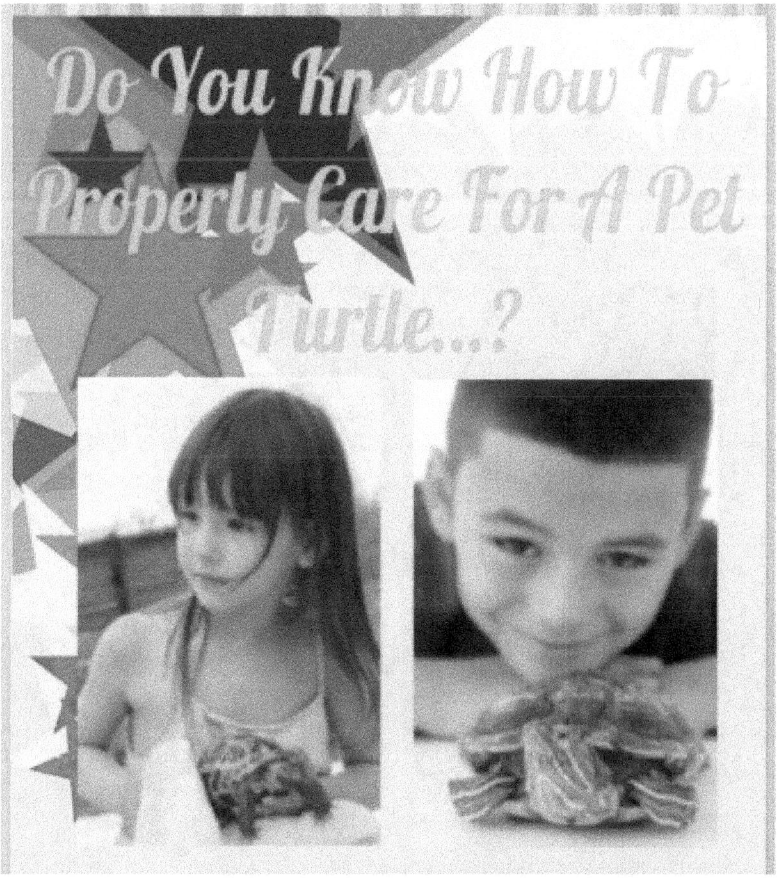
Do You Know How To
Properly Care For A Pet
Turtle...?

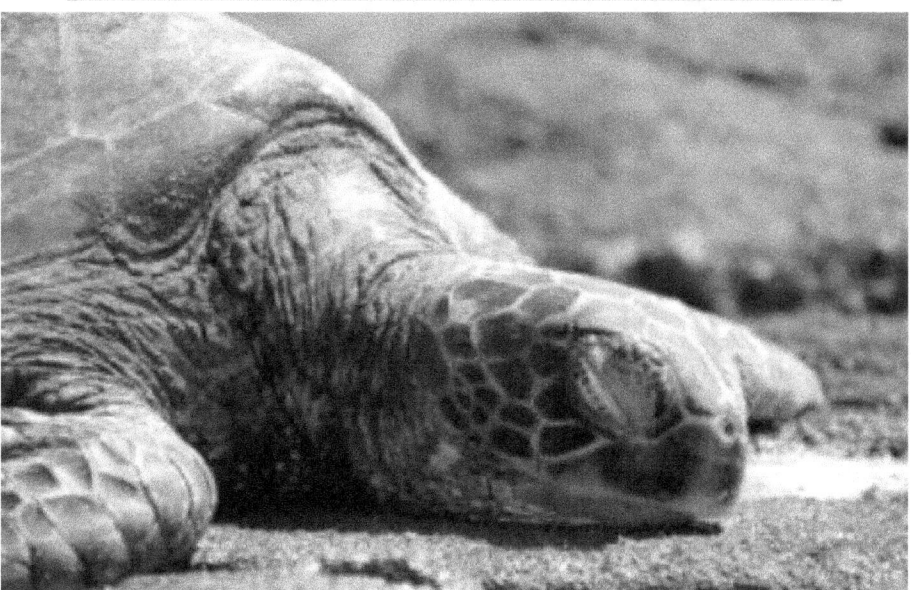

Funny that we don't have teeth! Isn't it...?

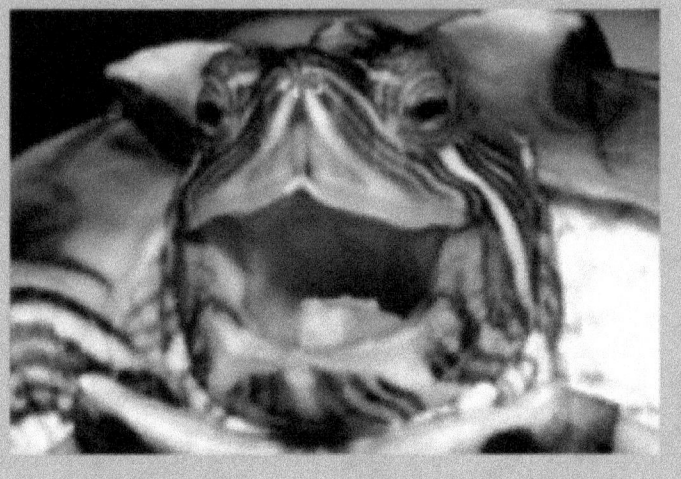

Don't We Have Beautiful Eyes...?

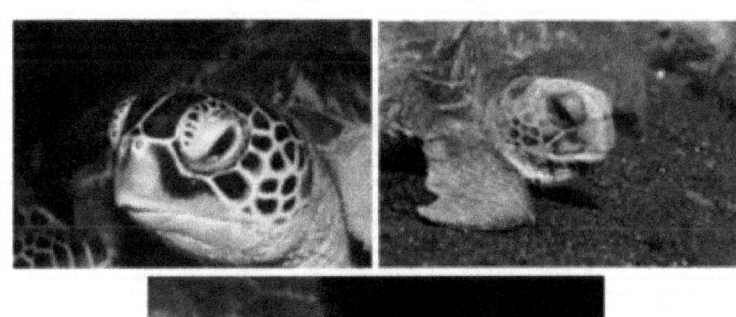
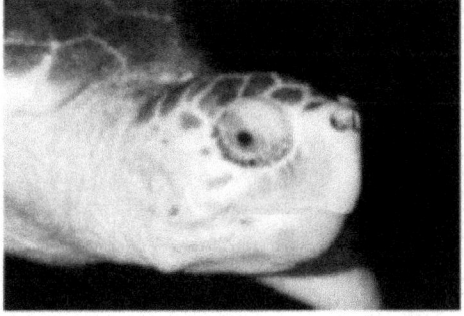

still sozializing...

Socializing...?

From the Carribean to the Shore of Key West...

The Navigation Ninjas...

This is How We Nest...

Yummie, this seaweed...

We are a real Sea Turtle Family

A little bit older, but still a lot to learn...

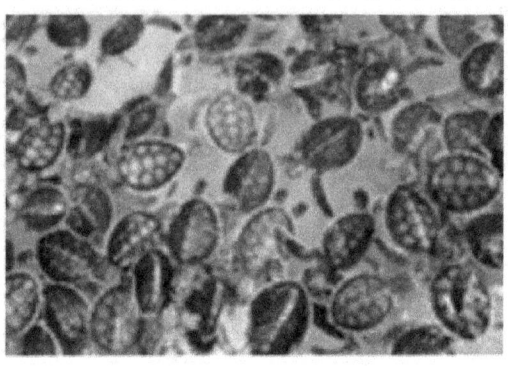

Finally, Here we are coming...

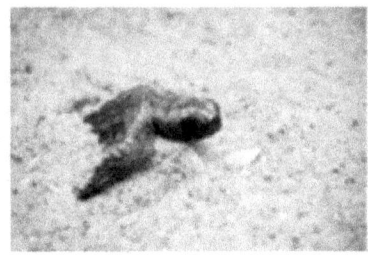

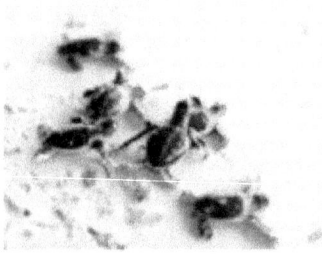
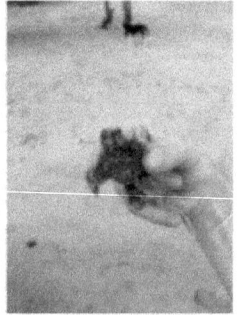

Soon the Turtle Babies will be there...

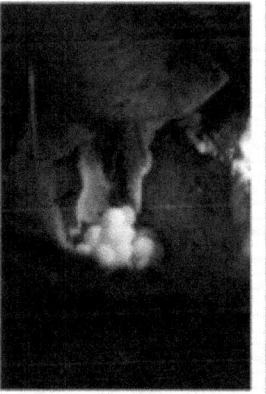

This is Exhausting, let's get some sleep...

Nesting...

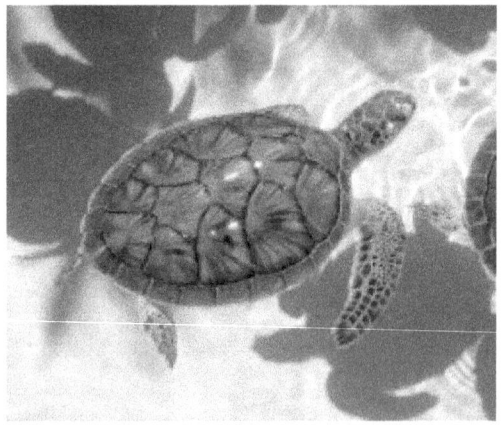

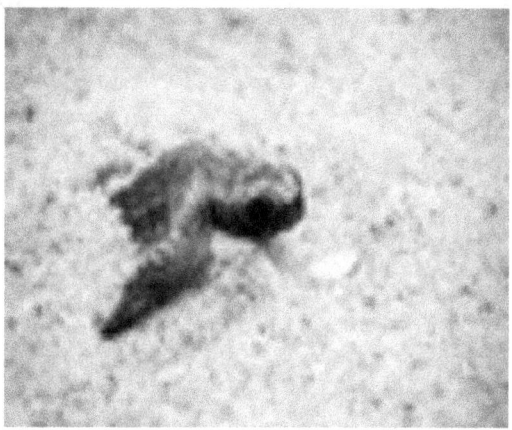

I am the African Helmeted Turtle

I am the Trionyx Cartilagineus

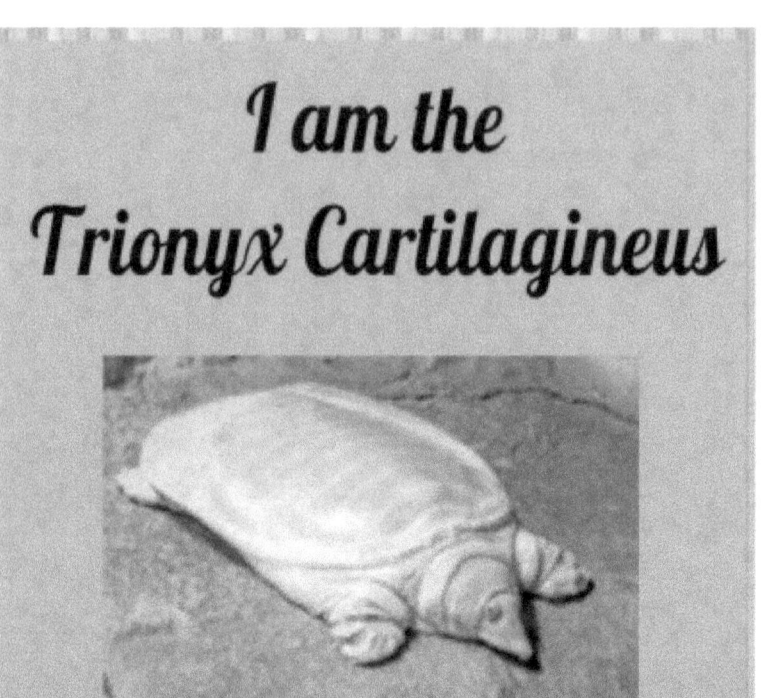

I am the Loggerhead Turtle...

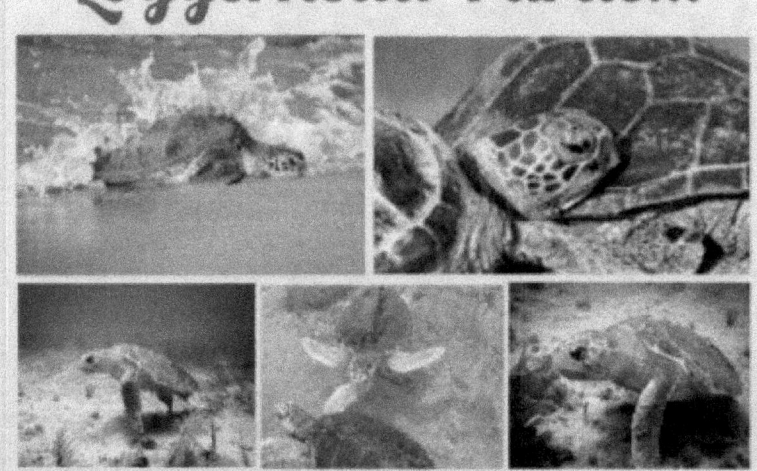

I am the Green Sea Turtle...

Look at me! I am the Beautiful Hawksbill...

I am the Olive Ridley

I am the Leatherback Turtle...

Hi there, I am the Snapping Turtle...

Try to be like the turtle - at ease in your own shell -- Bill Copeland

While every precaution has been taken in the preparation of this book, the publisher assumes no responsibility for errors or omissions, or for damages resulting from the use of the information contained herein.

SEATURTLE DISCOVERY KIDS: SEA STORIES OF CUTE SEA TURTLES WITH FUNNY PICTURES, PHOTOS & MEMES OF SEATURTLES FOR CHILDREN

First edition. July 31, 2017.

Copyright © 2017 Kate Cruso.

ISBN: 978-1540122261

Written by Kate Cruso.

My Favorite Sea Turtle Quote

Try to be like the turtle - at ease in your own shell -- Bill Copeland

Introduction

The reason why I wrote this sea turtle discover book as part of my "Discover Book Series" is an important one.

Every child should know about the issues that relate to sea turtles.

Did you know that in Indian mythology the sea turtle together with the elephant is one of the most powerful symbol? You will find out about this story in the chapter that talks about "Some Revelations, Truths & Other Curious Stuff About Sea Turtles!"

It is true the sea turtle is one of the most ancient species on the globe, but yet it is considered one of the endangered species today!

In a concerted effort we must all be aware of this fact and help to save it.

This book will provide your child with all the facts, stories, and pictures that are related to the sea turtle. Having a better understanding of who the sea turtle really is, from where it comes, and how it relates to us humans, your child will be able to have a better appreciation of the sea turtle and animals in general.

Your child will also discover many interesting, curious, and intriguing facts about the sea turtles which will in turn help your child appreciate its existence.

After having read the book your child will be better able to understand why the sea turtle is so precious to us humans and why we need to save its heritage.

By reading the book your child will personally get in touch with some amazing sea turtle moments and this alone is worth going through the discovery phase that this book is going to provide your child with.

In the end your child will know more cool things about the sea turtle and this knowledge will enrich your child on a mental level because knowledge is power.

If your child is an informed kid, he or she knows more stuff which in turn will enable him or her to get into a deeper discovery process and this in turn will help raise your child's interest level making him or her more involved and engaged in life in general.

This active mental discovery process will ultimately lead to a higher intelligence level.

Once your child is knowledgeable about the sea turtle, he or she can decide which way to go from here and he or she can truly start a positive mental relationship and friendship with this cute and peaceful swimming animal.

Who knows but maybe this information is going to be the basis for some of your kid's future initiatives. Based on information like this your child might engage his or her initiative for the cause of sea turtles or any other endangered animals at a later point in time.

Helping shape a positive future and helping shape the intelligence of responsible individuals who are going to care for extinct animals and who might one day bring their own resourcefulness, responsibility, and initiative to the table is part of the reason why I made it my mission to create this discovery series.

This sea turtle discovery book is the third volume within this discovery book series.

As a mother of twin boys and a little girl, I know that I want to be actively involved in their educational process to help shape their visions, imaginations, dreams, hopes, creativity, and their positive involvement with everything that this beautiful world of ours has to offer.

I have set my goal to help kids envision and discover intriguing, amazing, and curious stuff that they find cool and that is part of our life here on earth.

Encouraging them to view life from a totally new perspective and dimension helps kids build new mental connections between things that they might not have considered before is what I want to achieve with my books that I am writing for children about animals, nature, space, and other related issues.

Going through such an active discovery process helps stimulate the active thinking and contemplation process which in turn increases a child's intelligence in general.

Involving your child with a positive, creative, mentally involving and stimulating, interactive, and responsive educational discovery process where your kid gets satisfactory answers back is how you help shape the intelligence of your child.

If you are letting your child explore new and cool things about a subject you are making an active contribution into your child's future! Such an investment into your child's future is the most valuable investment that you can ever provide your child with.

This book will empower your child to raise and get answers for questions like why the sea turtle is endagnered, why the sea turtle is such an amazing animal, why it is important to save the sea turtle, what your child can do to help the sea turtle, and lots more.

These are just some more additional reasons why this sea turtle discovery book provides such an important contribution into your child's educational process and mental development.

Once your child is aware about all these issues that surround the sea turtle, he or she will feel more enriched and in tune with the nature, the world of the animals, our environment, and our earth.

Helping to protect the valuable species that have been brought to us by mother nature is one of our priorities as human beings.

We as human beings can create a healthy balance and we as human beings have the intelligence to create a balanced, protected, happy and peaceful life between humans and animals happen.

As you can see there are many reasons why reading this panda book is an important step into the future of your child.

I wrote the book in the most positive spirit and my main goal for the book can be summarized as follows.

As a mother it is my responsibility to entertain and engage my kids with positive educational content. In my opinion as a former first grade teacher,

mother nature provides the richest sources of valuable content for a child. Human beings, animals, and plants are a good way to get your child started with the discovery process.

My kids always tell me that they love to be entertained while they discover something new at the same time. Learning about some cool new information is how they learn best and they love to consume a mixture of pictures, funny facts, stories, and the curious and intriguing side of a specific animal or topic that they are learning about.

I know from my own experience as an educator and researcher and from my interaction with children in general that kids love to learn stuff the cool way.

I listened to kids and took the responses that I got from them and it is my goal to surprise them with a real cool book series. This discovery book series

is basically inspired by kids. It is made from kids for kids. It respects the way kids like to learn.

I created this book series in a way that respects the way how kids like to learn because they told me what they find cool and groovy and I listened to them and included it.

The book contains lots of pictures, cool facts, and other curious and intriguing stuff that kids just seem to be fascinated with.

This specific discovery book is about sea turtles and therefore it fulfills a second big goal. This book can also be seen as a contribution to help endangered sea turtles and to help stimulate children to contemplate about the endangered species of sea turtles.

This book should raise awareness about this endangered species in the eyes of a child. It should help a child be aware that it is possible between humans to sustainably coexist with sea turtles.

Lastly, I want to stress that this book is there to enrich your child's spirit, imagination, creativity, hope, dreams, and vision about the wonderful world of sea turtles.

A child must know that he or she has a stake in such a global cause like the sea turtles.

Reading about today's issues in such a positive and mentally stimulating way helps empower a kid's creativity, initiative, and interaction to create a better and happier future for a life in balance with the nature.

A child should also know that although the situation of the sea turtles is very delicate, there are positive news in regards to the recovery process of the sea turtle species because there are human beings who act in a very responsible way that helps sea turtles to sustain themselves in the nature by extending the nature reserves and by developing new projects and sea turtle protection programs to help human beings sustainably co exist and live in balance together with this endangered species - the sea turtle!

This is the result of joint effort between the CITES (short for The Convention on International Trade in Endangered Species Of Wild Fauna and Flora, some responsive governments and local communities and their initiatives, and responsible people like you and your child!

I truly hope that you and your child are going to enjoy the concept and the content of this book and I hope you get lots of valuable moments out of this discovery series.

I welcome every parent and child to discover the wonderful world of sea turtles - one of the oldest and most ancient species on earth, but sadly enough an endangered species at the same time!

What Is The History Behind The Origin Of Sea Turtles?

Life evolves by natural selection and with evolution we sea turtles have come a far way.

Did you know that we sea turtles are really ancient because we date back to the time of the first dinosaurs.

Sea turtles date back to the time of first dinosaurs, and there are as much turtles as any modern species is.

Although we are ancient and we date back to the dino days, hundreds of new sea turtle species have arisen since our early days.

We are also very proud of the fact that no lineage has lost our essential turtle heritage form.

We modern turtles are no 'fitter' or more powerful than our predecessors were. The only thing that distincts us between our ancestors is time and evolution.

Humans found pictures of our turtle ancestors on ancient cave walls which proves that we sea turtles are among the oldest creatures on earth and have remained essentially unchanged for 110 million years.

We the sea turtles are considered chelonians. We the sea turtles and the dinos emerged and developed at the same time.

The oldest known fossil turtle to man is the Odontochylys semitstacea. It dates back 220 million years in time. This turtle ancient turtle is extinct, but one thing is important to note about its appearance. It had a partial shell that covered the belly of this turtle. The shell did not extend to protect and shelter its back completely. Today, we chelonians have a complete protection by our shells.

You know what the most amazing thing is about us turtles? Even though some of us turtles existed millions of years ago, but their heritage is still around.

The Pelomedusidae turtle that is a family of freshwater turtles and that is native to southern and eastern Africa, made its first appearance around 120 million years ago and the first tortoise emerged on the land around 65 millions years ago. This happened after the dinosaurs died out via mass extinction.

The oldest surviving sea turtle species, the Cheloniidae, dates back around 55 million years.

Now these are some amazing turtle facts and who would have thought that turtles are nearly as old and ancient as dinos?

Well, I guess, our adventurous past kind of explains some of our weird behavior.

Sure, we turtles and tortoises alike are known to act pretty weird sometimes, but I guess we can justify it with our long history and so far we have been pretty successful with being able to adapt and to evolve - unlike many other species!

Here is what we are in a snapshot:

We are egg-laying, scaly reptiles and we do carry an oval shaped hard shell on top of us to protect us from intruders and enemies. The shell is pretty much where we feel at home and like humans have their house we have our house, too.

We are lumbering around in an incredible slow motion and speed and we have wrinkly skin, heads that are bald, and we pretty much look like wise old men - remember Yoda?

Hey, let's not forget our signature ability. We have a powerful ability to retract our wise little bold heads inside our shell and we do that when we do not have a clue what is going on and when we are frightened.

This is us and we sea turtles have brought our ancient herritage to these modern days and we are pretty proud of our evolution!

Below you can see us in one of our favorite positions and that is: SLEEPING ON THE SURFACE OF THE WATER!

Well, know that you know a little bit more about who we are and where we come from, let's jump to the next chapter where we tell you one of our next big secret: Why we are different from Tortoises!

How Is A Sea Turtle Different From A Tortoise?

You probably might have seen us sea turtles in action, but you still might be confused because you might also have come in contact with tortoises.

This is what brings us to the next important question.

What is the difference between a sea turtle and a tortoise?

I am glad you asked...Tortoises and Turtles are both reptiles from the family of Testudines.

What are Testudines? Well, we turtles are reptiles of the Chelonii or Testudines order and this is how we are also referred to as Testudines.

The major difference that you have to take a look on is the following. The land dwelling creatures are called Tortoises and the water dwelling creatures are called turtles or more specifically sea turtles.

We sea turtles love to be in contact with water and we need water to be able to survive. Our whole life is dependent on the existance of water.

As we turtles do live in water, our shell is different as opposed to a tortoise.

Our shell is flat and streamlined which aids in swimming and diving while that of a Tortoise, which lives on land, is rather large and dome shaped to provide protection from the predators.

The shell of a tortoise is heavier as compared to that of a turtle.

Our shell is much lighter and the reason for this is a physical one.

Turtoises do not live in water so they do not mind to carry a heavier shell that they call their home.

We as sea turles do need a lighter shell to avoid sinking and to help us swim faster in the water.

Most land-based tortoises are herbivores while we turtles can be both herbivores and carnivores.

Above you can see a Young African Sulcata tortoise and below is a A Red-Eared Slider Turtle with eyes closer to the end of the head, keeping only the nostrils and the eyes above the water surface...

What Are The Various Turtle Species?

Did you know that there are many breeds of sea turtles all around the world? Below you will find some of our various turtle breeds. Maybe you can even reckognize some of our breeds...

Do You know me....

...Well, I think that I am the most beautiful sea turtle! Don't you agree...?

You are telling me that You Did Not Know That I look like a Sea Turtle?

Well, let me introduce myself...

I am the prey luring "Alligator Snapping Turtle" and I am the most dangerous sea turtle because I am luring for prey with my tongue!

Below you will find some other sea turtle breeds...

Today, there are 250 species of us sea turtles in existence. We vary in our favorite locations, our size, our diet, and many other physical features. Our size varies and it depends upon our species.

We consist of species like the Small Kemp's Ridley. This is a large species because the Small Kemp Ridley can weigh between 80-100 pounds. However, the Small Kemp Ridley is nothing in terms of weight as opposed to the enormous Leatherback.

The Leatherback is enormous and it can weigh more than 1,000 pounds. In this chapter we are going to look at 10 different turtle species.

- **The Alligator Snapping Turtle**
- **Snapping Turtle**
- **Leatherback**
- **Olive ridley**
- **Kemp's ridley**
- **Hawksbill**
- **The Green Sea Turtle**
- **Loggerhead**
- **The Trionyx Cartilagineus Turtle**
- **The African Helmeted Turtle**

Snapping Turtle

One of the most fearsome breed around the globe is the "Alligator Snapping Turtle". It is also known under the name "Macroclemys Temminckii". This is the biggest freshwater turtle in North America.

It is huge and can truly grow as long as 2.5 feet long. It can weigh as much as 200 pounds. This turtle has a very powerful jaw. It also carries a sharply hooked beak and some nasty bearlike claws. It is supported by a very muscular tail.

Yes, the alligator snapping turtle does not kid around. It still eats some aquatic and underwater plants, but this turtle can also turn into a dangerous carnivore. This carnivore is able to dine on a bunch of small creatures. It loves eating frogs, fish, snakes, clams, worms, crayfish, clams, and even other crayfish and even some other and weaker turtles than themselves.

Prey catching for the snapping turtle happens like this. The snapping turtle uses a fiendishly clever evolutionary adaptation. This turtle uses an appendage to its tongue.

When the trutle wriggles the tongue it looks almost like a worm. A fish might get fooled and confuses the tongue with a worm. The fish will swim towards the enemy and this hungry predator's jaws and gets eaten alive.

Leatherback

The Leatherback is named for its unique shell. The shell is composed of a layer of thin, tough, and rubbery skin. The shell is strengthened by thousands of tiny bone plates that make it look "leathery."

Description: The head of the Leatherback has a deeply notched upper jaw with 2 cusps. The leatherback is the only sea turtle that lacks a hard shell and is composed of a layer of thin, tough, rubbery skin and strengthened by thousands of tiny bone plates. All flippers are without claws

Size: The adult Leatherback has a size of 4 to 6 feet (130 - 183 cm)

Weight: The adult Leatherback weighs 660 to 1,100 pounds (300 - 500 kg)

Olive ridley

picture source: Bernard Gagnon

This sea turtle carries the name Olive Ridley becaus it is named for its olive green coloured shell.

Description: Its head is quite small. Its body is deeper than the very similar Kemp's Ridley sea turtle. Both the front and rear flippers have 1 or 2 visible claws. Juveniles are charcoal grey in color, while adults are a dark grey green color

Hatchlings are black when they are wet and they have greenish sides

Size: Adult Olive Ridleys measure 2 to 2.5 feet (62-70 cm) in carapace length

Weight: Adult Olive Ridleys weigh between 77 and 100 pounds (35-45 kg)

Kemp's ridley

source: U.S. Fish and Wildlife Service
Southeast Region

Kemp's Ridley Nesting...

This turtle is named Kemp Ridley after Richard Kemp, who helped discover and study this species of turtle. No one is sure why it is called Ridley, possibly due to having similar nesting behaviour as the Olive Ridley Turtle.

Description: The Kemp Ridley's head is moderate and triangular in size. Its front flippers have 1 claw, while the rear flipper has 1 or 2 claws. Adult Kemp Ridleys have a dark grey green carapace with a white or yellowish plastron, while the hatchlings are jet black.

Size: Adult Kemp Ridleys measure around 2 feet (58 - 66 cm) in average carapace length.

Weight: Adult Kemp Ridleys weigh between 70 and 108 pounds (32 - 49 kg).

Hawksbill

source: magicOlf

The Hawksbill is named for its narrow head and hawk-like beak.

Description: The Hawksbill is one of the smaller sea turtles in existence. The Hawksbill's head is narrow. The flippers have 2 claws. The carapace of the Hawksbill is orange, brown, or yellow. Hatchlings are mostly brown with pale blotches on scutes.

Size: Adult Hawksbills are 2.5 to 3 feet in carapace length (71 - 89 cm).

Weight: Adult Hawksbills can weigh between 101 and 154 lbs (46 - 70 kg).

Green Sea Turtle

Source: Alexander Vasenin

The green sea turtle is named for its green color of the fat under its shell. (In some areas, for example, the Pacific green turtle is also called the black sea turtle.)

Description: These Green Sea Turtles are easily distinguished from other sea turtles. They have only a single pair of prefrontal scales (scales in front of its eyes), rather than two pairs as found on other sea turtles. Their head is small and blunt with a serrated jaw. The body of the Green Sea Turtle is nearly oval and is more depressed (flattened). All four flippers have 1 visible claw.

Size: Adult Green Sea Turtles are 3 to 4 feet in carapace length (83 - 114 cm).

Weight: Adult Green Sea Turtles weigh between 240 and 420 pounds (110 - 190 kg).

Loggerhead

Source: ukanda

The Loggerhead is named for its exceptionally large head.

Description: The Loggerhead's head is very large with a heavy strong jaws. The turtle's front flippers are short and thick with 2 claws, while the rear flippers can have 2 or 3 claws. The carapace of the Loggerhead is a reddish-brown with a yellowish-brown plastron. Loggerhead hatchlings have a dark-brown carapace with flippers pale brown on margins.

Size: Typically 2.5 to 3.5 feet in carapace length (80-110 cm).

Weight: Adult weigh between 155 and 375 pounds (70 -0 170 kg).

The Trionyx Cartilagineus Turtle

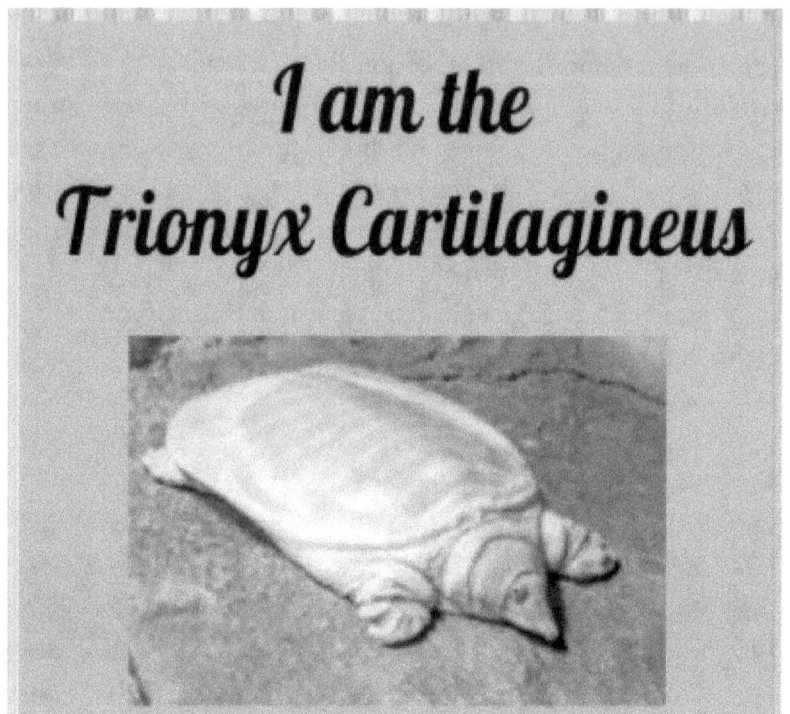

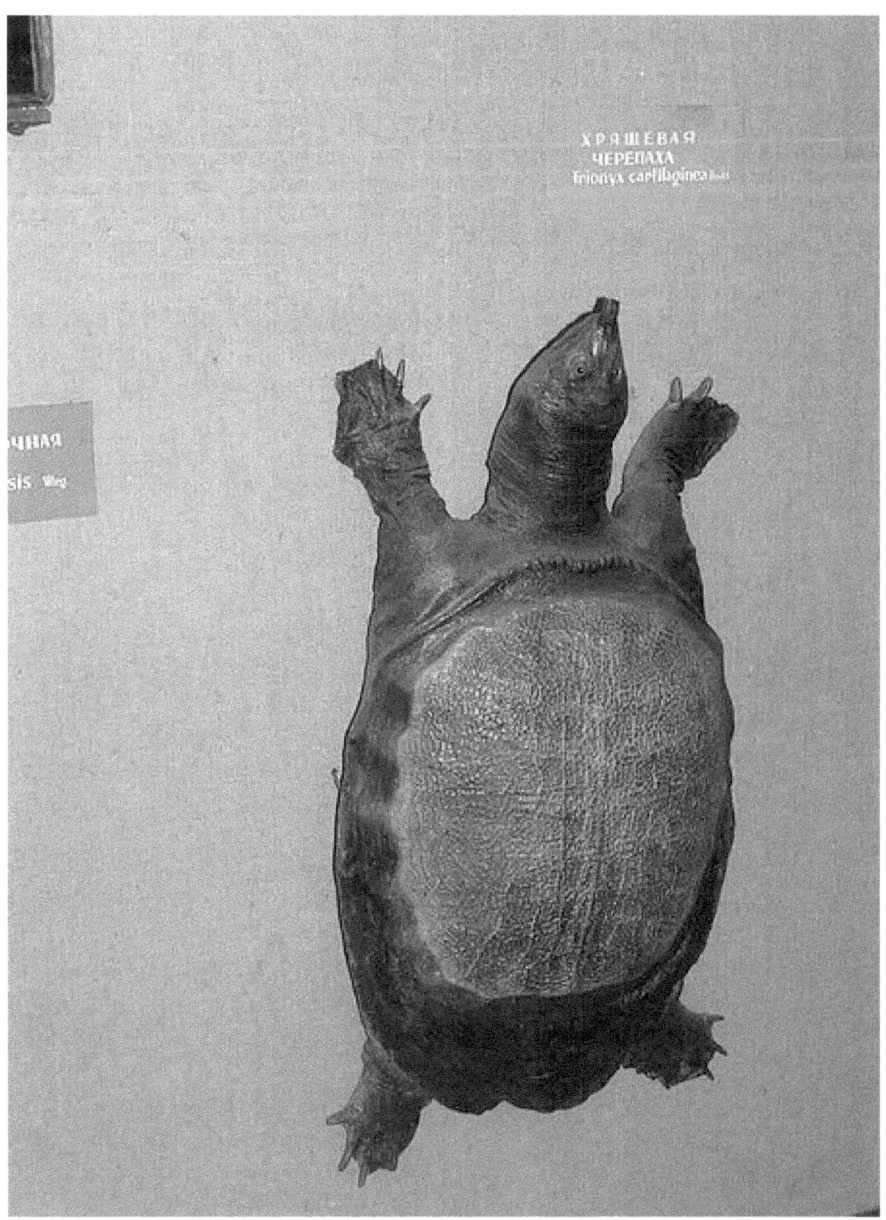

source: This photograph was created by Andrew Butko

The African Helmeted Turtle

Did you know that there are sea turtles that seem part skunk among us turtles? If so then you probably already know about the african helmeted turtle that is yet another turtle species.

The African helmeted turtle is also called the Pelomedusa subrufa.

It is the most widespread turtle species in Africa, too.

The African helmeted turtle or the Pelomedusa subrufa is found in the south of the Sahara desert.

This turtle species is a more of a hunter scavenger unlike the rest of us.

The African helmeted turtle hunts in packs and seems very happy to devour everything from young birds, small mammals, and parasites lodged in the skin of rhinoceroses.

This turtle even attacks ducklings. The African helmeted turtle drags the ducklings underwater. It also steals bait from anglers' hooks so that the anglers have no clue what just happened.

The Africans who get regularly in contact with this "Ninja" turtle dislike the turtle's immoral eating habits.

This turtle has not a very good reputation among Africans, but it gets even worse because stealing and drowning is not the only immoral behavior that this relative of ours demonstrates.

Can you believe this! This African relative of ours is producing a smelly and flatulent odour that is almost disgusting. Yes, this turtle is really an exceptional creature and has nothing in common with the good manners that most of us sea turtles are known for.

As you can imagine there is a reason for this stinky smell. You probably might be thinking that a stinky, farty, and poopy turtle is funny, but the reason for this flatulent smell is a very natural one and has to do with protection, self defense, and survival.

The stinky smell comes from the turtles's glands that are under each flipper. The glands do release a foul/flatulent smelling liquid. This aroma not only repulses humans, but it repulses other animals like horses, too.

African villagers, however, have the habit to dig up these turtles from their mud nest during the wet seasons for food even though they despise the unpleasant turtle odor that comes from this smelly shelled creatures.

I guess these villagers have not yet heard about our protection program that has been founded by the CITES (short for The Convention on International Trade in Endangered Species Of Wild Fauna and Flora) and which interdicts the trade of us sea turtles. The CITES bans any activities that do involve us sea turtles in a threatening and harmful way worldwide.

Well, if you'd like to learn more about the dangers that we face on a daily basis, please make sure to refer to the chapter: "Is The Future Of Sea Turtles In Danger?"

Thanks for your help and support so that we do not have to face extinction!

Sea Turtle's Shape, Size, Color & Other Body Features

We sea turtles come in many shapes, sizes, colors, and forms and we have served as models for art, fashion, design, architecture, and many other disciplines over the years. Humans admire our beauty and strenghts and they take us as a source of inspiration to come up with their own interpretation and use our beautiful heritage as source for their creativity.

We come in various different sizes, colors, and shapes. The olive ridley, one of our species, for example weighs usually less than 100 pounds, while the leatherback, another breed, typically ranges from 650 to 1,300 pounds. What a difference in weight!

The upper shell, or carapace, of each of us sea turtle species ranges in color, length, shape, arrangement, and design of scales. Our shell makes us turtles so powerful and ancient looking! Our shell protection, body functions, adaptability, and flexibililty is part of the reason why we have been able to surve until modern days.

We sea turtles are also characterized by a large and streamlined shell design.

Depending on the species you are looking at, we sea turtles also range in various colors. We may range from colors that go from olive-green, yellow, greenish-brown to the darkest color of black.

Our large and bony shell provides us with the necessary protection so that no predation and abrasion can happen to us. We sea turtles can not retract our limbs and our head under our shell. Land turtles and turtoises for example can do that.

We sea turtles, however, have large upper eyelids that provide protection for our eyes.

We sea turtles do not even have an external ear opening! Can you imagine?

Like other creatures, we sea turtles lack teeths as well and we still have been able to survive!

Our jaw shape might be different among us different sea turtle species. Each of our species has a jaw shape that is adequately adapted for its specific diet and food consumption.

Our tough shell helps us act as a protection shield or an external armour against any potential threats, predators, and enemies.

Our shell provides us with a very useful defence mechanism.

We can protect ourselves with our powerful jaws to make sure that we stay here on earth and do not get extinct like it already happened with so many other animals.

Some other things you might consider about our shell because our shell is our most importatn armor.

Our shell is made up of around fifty bones. They are all different. Basically our shell is an evolutionary modification. It is our rib cage and part of our vertebral column. Our shell has two parts and it consists of the upper and the lower part. The upper part is called the carapace and the lower is called the pastron. Both parts are joined by a bridge made of bones.

Some of us turtles do have a moveable joint so that we are able to squeeze our two parts tightly together in order to retract our body inside.

Unbelievable but true, but our hard shells even have nerves embedded into it. Blood supply also

Shells have nerves embedded in them and a blood supply as well because like stated earlier the shell of a sea turtle is what a vertebral column is to us humans.

This is why a chelonian's shell like ours may bleed and we may feel pain if our shell is injured.

As you can see, we have pretty amazing body features and our shell armor is pretty ninja don't you agree?

So make sure to check us out at your next visit to the zoo or at an exotic vacation that you might take with your parents because we might be able to teach you some amazing stuff about life, nature, and survival!

Make sure to take a look on our beauty, body features and functions, and shell armor.

Once you change your perspective and view the world from our perspective, you can find out many incredible things and wonders about us sea turtles.

Once you know about our secrets, you will understand why we have been able to carry our heritage from one generation over to the next generation and why we are still here!

Yes, we turtles survived and evolved over 110 million years. Our shell (our home), our anatomy, as well as a mixture of other things that we know how to do like true ninjas has helped us evolve and stay here on earth as a living animal.

If you are taking a very close look at us, you might get many more of your questions answered and find out more about our survival skills and secrets.

Once you got all your questions answered about us sea turtles, you might have a better understanding of who we really are!

One of your many questions about us sea turtles is the question: "How do sea turtles mate and how do sea turtle babies (hatchlings) look like?" You will get this question answered in the next chapter.

Oh, and here you can see us coming out of the sea and getting ready for

nesting. Aren't our babies the hatchlings cute?

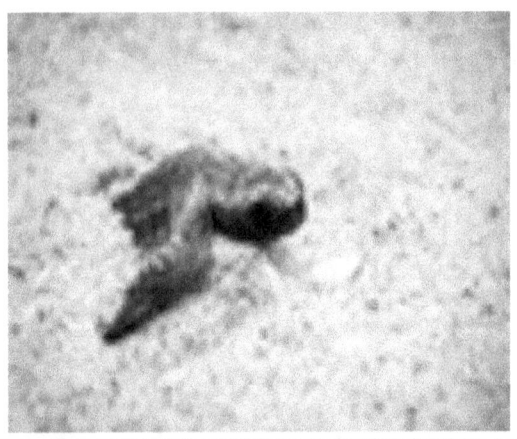

Here you can see some more facettes of us Sea Turtles...

Aren't we true creatures of beauty...?

How Do Sea Turtles Reproduce? How Do Sea Turtle Babies Look Like?

We sea turtles usually mate during a very limited "receptive" period of time.

After the mating process only the females of our species come ashore to nest.

Males never return to shore once they leave the sand of their natal beach as a hatchling.

In addition to choosing a very limited period of time during mating, our methods and behaviors become even a bit weirder.

During mating season, males may court a female by nuzzling her head or by gently biting the back of her neck and rear flippers.

A bit weird! Isn' it?

We male chelonians love sniffing under the female chelonians' tails and this is how we begin the mating process.

This is a is a very sensible area because our sexual organs are hidden inside the male's and female's cloaca.

This is a cavity used for both reproduction and eliminating waste, too. I told you that we are some weird animals, but at the same time we have been able to survive as opposed to the dinos!

I guess we really survived because of our smart functionality and flexibility!

We Turtles and the tortoises as well do possess an extremely sensitive sense of smell.

Male turtles can detect the scent of pheromones. Pheromones are a type of chemical which is secreted inside the female turtle's cloaca.

Chelonians like us primarily rely on scent heavily.

Funny but true story:

Once a male red footed tortoise was observed by some human beings and the tortoise was trying to mount a head of lettuce that a female tortoise had just left! This demonstrates just how heavily we sea turtles depend on scent.

Here is what happens next after the mating phase.

Female turtles can be observed on the nesting beach.

Most females return faithfully to the same beach each time they are ready to nest.

There is a very specific ritual that our female sea turtles go through when they are crawling out of the ocean in order to get ready to nest.

The female turtles are pausing frequently as if carefully scoping out the perfect spot for the nest. The female turtle is crawling to a dry part of the beach and begins to fling away loose sand with her flippers. She then starts constructing a "body pit" by digging with her flippers and by rotating her body.

After she has completed her body pit, she is digging an egg cavity using her upped rear flippers as shovels. When the female turtle has finished digging her egg chamber, she begins the proces of laying her eggs.

Once all her eggs are in the chamber, the mother turtle uses her rear flippers to push a load of sand over the top of the egg cavity. Gradually, she packs the sand down over the top and then begins using her front flippers to refill the body pit and disguise her nest so that enemies can not find it.

By throwing sand in all directions, it is much harder for predators to find her eggs.

After the nest is thoroughly concealed, the female turtle crawls back from where she came from earlier. She has to rest in the sea before nesting again at a later point in time.

Once a female tuttle has left her nest, she never returns to tend it because nature is doing the rest of the work for her.

The temperature, for example, governs the speed at which the embryos are going to develop; the hatching period can cover a broad range.

Essentially, the hotter the grains of the sand surrounding her nest, the faster the embryos are goig to develop.

Hatchlings are smart creatures already because they are able to break up their shells by using a temporary, sharp egg tooth. This egg tooth is called the "caruncle". The hatchlings are only using this tool for braking free from their shell and the egg tooth falls off soon after their birth.

Digging out of the nest is an effort that the small hatchlings can only achieve by using a powerful group effort.

This process can take them several days.

Hatchlings usually achieve this group effort successfully and they emerge tothether from their nest at night time or during a rainstorm when temperatures are much cooler which helps them survive during their weakest time as a hatchling.

Once their instinct tells them to burst out, they erupt from the nest cavity together as a group for more protection.

The little turtles instinctively orient themselves to the brightest light of the horizon, and this is where they keep dashing toward the sea.

Yes, these sea turtle hatchlings love the moonlight and phosphorescence from the ocean.

Once in the ocean, the little hatchlings are swimming to the gulf stream to eat sargassum sea weed. They also use this sea weed for protection and shelter. Our little hatchlings also love to eat baby shrimps or jellyfish. Hatchlings will also return to the exact same beach from where they were born.

Here you can see the many facettes of us Sea Turtles in groups because we like to stay in groups as hatchlings and until adulthood...

A little bit older, but still a lot to learn...

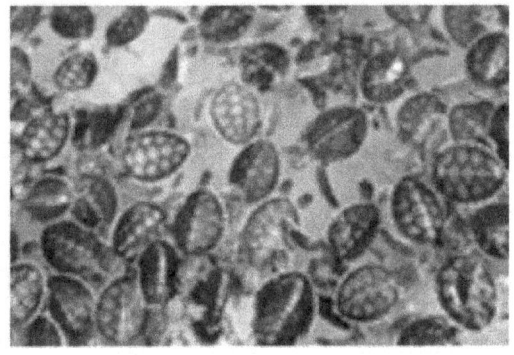

We are a real Sea Turtle Family

If they are making it to adulthood, they will nest there like their mother before them did. It is a very true and very sad fact that only one hatchling out of 1,000 will survive to adulthood.

The 999 others will not make it to that beach because they were either killed by natural causes or by human and artificial causes like I am going to tell you about in the chapter: "Is The Future Of Sea Turtles In Danger?"

Before we are going to the more serious stuff though, let's first learn more about what we do and how we behave so that you can better an even better understanding of who we really are first.

What Behaviors Do Sea Turtles Show?

Swimming

We sea turtles love swimming with the help of our flippers. Our flippers are adapted for swimming. We sea turtles are awkward and vulnerable on land because our flippers are only adapted to work well in water.

We sea turtles do have a carapace or upper shell that is streamlined to help us swimming and keep us from drowning.

We also have a lower shell, called a plastron. In all but one species, the carapace is covered in hard scutes.

Unlike land turtles, we sea turtles can not retreat into our shells. We have paddle-like flippers. While our flippers are great for propelling us through the water, we are poorly-suited for walking on land.

We are alos breathing air. This is why we sea turtles must come to the water surface when we need to breathe some fresh air.

Some of us sea turtles have special muscles to help us with breathing. Some of us sea turtles have developed a certain breathing trick that allows us to stay under water for very long time periods.

Some of us turtles also use buccopharyngeal breathing. What is buccopharyngeal breathing? Well, with this type of breating the turtle takes water into the mouth and passes it out of the nostrils. The oxygenated water then can pass along the turtle's capillary rich tissues inside the neck. This allows for additional oxygen intake that enters directly into the turtle's bloodstream.

Many of us turtles, however, have to come up to the surface of the sea to take some fresh air and this is the moment where we turtles are most vulnerable to boats that crash into us and hurt us!

Swimming is our favorite activity and we can swim from Aruba to Key West...

If you don't believe me that we are strong swimmers, here is an amzing turtle story for you that proves my point. I call this story the "Ninja Turtle Swimming Journey From Aruba to Key West" and it happened to one of my sea turtle buddies.

Here is the story and I hope you find it as hilarious as we turtles do.

When Mister Dick de Bruin, a man from a Dutch speaking country, dropped his video camera by accident while he was diving in the Carribean, more specifically near the shore of Aruba, he probably thought: "I am in bad luck today!"

No, Mister Dick de Bruin, you are wrong because bad luck does not exist for us sea turtles.

We sea turtles are only in bad luck if we are bumping into some people who do not care about us, but within our own sphere and protected by the laws of mother nature we are very lucky animals!

Anyways, his assumptions were wrong because he did not imagine that we sea turtles might actually help him and make him lucky again!

Guess what happened, folks!

One of our species ran into his waterproof video camera and this sea turtle showed some interest for the Dutchman's underwater video camera and while inspecting the object became entangled with it. Probably the turtle became tangled around its shell.

It gets even funnier because 6 months after the loss of the camera, the device got found at a Florida beach and thousands of miles away from where the loss happened.

The sea turtle was so smart it even inadvertently switched on the video camera to capture parts of this legendary thousand mile journey for everyone to see.

The swimming trip from Aruba to Florida happened live on camera and is now on record for everyone to enjoy!

There was even more luck involved in this whole story because not only did the lost camera got found by this interested sea turtle, but it also got found on a beach in Florida, where the sea turtle left it after the exhausting trip from the Carribean to the shore of Florida, six months after the Dutchman lost it under water close to the shore of Aruba.

The camera finally got found by US Coast Guard officer, Paul Shultz, who identified and found the device during one of his duties at the beach in Key West. He charged the batteries and was able to operate the camera in order to find the person who lost it.

Paul Shultz was struck by a surprise when he found out the real proof of what happened to the camera and who lost it. He found out that the true hero of the story was not a human being, but a sea turtle and he also found out about how the camera got transported from Aruba to Florida.

By watching the entire film, Paul Shultz found out that the camera belongs to someone who vacationed in Aruba because the proof of all the vacation photos plus the aquatic sea turtle adventure that was filmed by the sea turtle was all captured by the same camera.

The most funny part, however, is that the story got so lucky that the Dutchman was able to find his camera via a video that he found on Youtube because Paul Shultz put the film on Youtube in order to find the Dutchman who lost the camera while he was scuba diving in Aruba.

There happened even more luck the the dutchman because he really saw the video of the turtle who carried his video camera across the sea

and Paul Shultz's note that Paul added as a description to the video (which kind of reminds me of the most modern type of a message in the bottle).

Once Mr. Bruin, the dutchman got in contact with Paul Shultz, the officer told him about this amazing challenge and the journey that the sea turtle took with his camera. Mr Shultz told Mr. Bruin that the last part of the camera's trip back to the owner is going to take place not by snail mail but by Fed-Ex.

This is how the camera that was lost in Aruba got back to the the real owner who lost it there over 6 months ago by accident and during his snorkeling trip under water.

This is such a funny story that is full of so many touching and lucky moments and it helps show and prove that nature and animals on one side should always be able to live together in co-existence with human beings because this is the only way that will ever produce a lucky outcome for the animals and for the human beings together!

Make sure to read some other funny and intriguing stories about us sea turtles in chapter: "Some Revelations, Truths & Other Curious Stuff About Sea Turtles!" where you will find out about a very curious and mystic Indian saying about us sea turtles. This saying is part of the Indian mythology and it is a very wise saying. I am sure that you are going to like it!

Eating

We turtles are not strictly herbivores. All species are found to eat at least some meat which causes them to have powerful digestive enzymes. In addition we turtles do swallow our food with almost no chewing. Food particles are often whole or in fairly large chunks. Our salivary glands help us to soften and break down the food to make swallowing possible.

Our diet depends upon the species. Some of us are omnivores, eating a variety of plants and animals, while the Hawksbill for example and the Leatherback are specialists, subsisting primarily of sponges (hawksbills) and jellyfish (leatherbacks).

Some of us sea turtles undertake impressive migrations to find food that we like and we are known to cross the entire Pacific Ocean just to find swarms of jellyfish...!

Nest Building

Look at how some of our females build their nests...

Only our females go ahead and nest. Most often this nesting process takes place during the night when it is cooler.

The female crawls out of the ocean, pausing frequently as if she is carefully scoping out her perfect nesting spot.

Sometimes she will crawl out of the ocean, but for unknown reasons decide not to nest there and find another place.

This is also called a "false crawl," and it can happen naturally or be caused by artificial lighting or the presence of people on the beach.

Most of our female sea turtles do nest at least twice during the nesting season, although individuals of some species may nest only once and others more than ten times.

We sea turtles are generally slow and awkward on land, and nesting is exhausting work from our perspective of things.

Navigation

The Navigation Ninjas...

In the open ocean, we sea turtles encounter strong currents.

One of our weaknesses is that we only have a modest vision.

We can only raise our head several inches out of the water, and there are often no visible landmarks.

Even with these limitations, we sea turtles regularly navigate long distances to find the same tiny stretch of nesting beach.

How we are capable to do this is one of our greatest mysteries and secrets in the world of animals.

We do not easily divulge this type of classified information to the human beings because this remains one of our top secrets and maybe you will find it out some day.

I told you that we are weird little animals before, but on top of it we are smart and wise and this type of secret classified information is the type of stuff that has helped us survive as a species.

Finding an answer to this secret has been the focus of generations of researchers, but they still have not been able to find out about our secret ninja navigation stuff.

Migration

...and we are real Nomands and we can travel 1.300 Miles per day!

From the Carribean to the Shore of Key West...

When it is not nesting season, we sea turtles may migrate hundreds or even thousands of miles.

We sea turtles can sleep at the surface of the water while in deep water or on the bottom wedged under rocks in nearshore waters.

Many divers have seen some of our green turtles sleeping under ledges in reefs and rocks. Hatchlings typically sleep floating on the surface, and they usually have their front flippers folded back over the top of their backs.

Can you imagine how cute this must look like in reality?

Are Sea Turtles Carnivore, Herbivore, Or Omnivore? What Do The Sea Turtles Eat?

Depending on the species, sea turtles may be carnivorous (meat eating), herbivorous (plant eating), or omnivorous (eating both meat and plants). The jaw structure of many of us sea turtle species is adapted for our specific diets and each different sea turtle species has a different diet.

Green sea turtles, for example, do have fine serrated jaws (pretty much saw-like) adapted for a vegetarian diet of sea grasses and algae.

This also allows them to scrape algae off rocks and tear grasses and seaweeds.

Greens sea turtles, for example, find food (forage) among beds of seagrass and within habitats that are near the shore.

Some species change eating habits as they age. For example, green sea turtles are mainly carnivorous from hatching until juvenile size. They then

progressively shift and turn their diet into a pure herbivorous diet.

A Hawksbill sea turtle on the other side has a very narrow head with jaws and eats sponges, squids, tunicates, and shrimps.

Loggerheads' and Ridleys' jaws, for example, are adapted for crushing and grinding food and therefore their diet consists primarily of molluscs, crabs, jellyfish, shrimps, and vegetation.

Leatherbacks have delicate scissor-like jaws that would be damaged by anything other than their normal diet that consists of sea food like tunicates, jellyfish, and other soft-bodied animals.

In a zoological environment all sea turtle species can be maintained and taken care of by feeding them with a carnivorous diet.

The next time you are going to visit the zoo make sure to watch out for us sea turtles and to discover in real time how we are foraging (finding food), approaching food, and devouring food!

What Are The Senses In Sea Turtles? How Do They Communicate?

You may have heard people say that we turtles and the tortoises as well lack an ear opening and are deaf. This statement is not entirely true. It is true that we chelonians can not hear anywhere near as well as human beings and many other species can. However, we chelonians can detect certain types of sounds.

Researcher have found out about us that our middle ears have a very thick eardrum-like membrane, which limits the frequency range that we can perceive.

Chelonians like us generally can perceive sounds in the 50 to 1,500 Hz range, compared to the typical human hearing range of 20 to 20,000 Hz.

We hard-shelled chelonians, for example, can not differentiate loudness. The spotted turtle (Clemmys guttata) that you can see blow, for example, has a peak sensitivity of just 4 dB (decibel).

The decibel is a logarithmic unit and it is used in physics. The decibel (dB) is used to show the ratio between two values of a physical quantity.

The decibel is used for a wide variety of measurements in science and engineering. These sciences are most prominently in electronics, acoustics, and control theory.

The spotted turtle (Clemmys guttata)

Sense of touch

We sea turtles are very sensitve to touch and particularly on the softer parts of our flippers and on our shell.

Sense of taste

Little is known by researchers about our sense of taste!

Sense of smell

Most researchers believe that we have an acute sense of smell in water. Experiements with us sea turtles show that our hatchlings do react to the scent of shrimps. The adaptation helps us sea turtles to locate our food in murky water.

We only open our mouth slightly and we draw in water through our nose. We then immediately empty the water out again and through our mouth.

The pulsating movements of our throat are thought to be associated with smelling by researchers.

Sense of hearing

All reptiles, including us sea turtles, have a single bone in the middle ear that conducts vibrations to the inner ear. Researchers have found that we sea turtles respond to low frequency sounds and vibrations.

Sense of sight

Sea turtles like us can see well under water, but we are short-sighted in the air.

Communication

Under experimental conditions, our species like the Loggerhead and the Green Sea Turtle hatchlings are exhibiting a preference for near-ultraviolet, violet, and blue-green light.

Scientists believe that we sea turtles communicate by making sounds. With these sounds, we are able to find each other. We also bite each other and make bobbing head movements when trying to mate.

Are Sea Turtles Social?

You wanna know if we sea turtles are good at social interaction with each other?

Well, let me tell you this.

We sea turtles are not generally considered social animals like pandas for example. Pandas are much cuter and social than us because they play together and eat together.

We on the other hand are a bit more complex when it comes to social activities. Some species of us for example do like to congregate offshore and we sea turtles only gather together in a social way to mate.

There are members of some species that travel together to nesting grounds.

After the hatchlings reach the water they generally remain solitary and as a group until they mate which can be interpreted as a social activity, too.

Our instincts know that this is the way how we need to do things and evolution has taught us that we can only survive as a species if we keep doing things the way we have been doing things for millions of years.

We might be a little bit weird and do things differently and humans might think we are crazy freaks, but this is just the way that has proven itself to work for us.

Guess what!

Our success in staying alive and not becoming extinct tells us that our weirdness kind of pays off and our results show that we have been doing the right things. The natural threats that we are constantly bombarded with have not caused our extinction so far, but the human interaction if it is harmful to us might cause our extinction one day!

At least for now we have been proven that the way we do things works because we have been able to survive extinction, but the future will show where we are in a couple of years...

Do Turtles Have Favorite Colors?

Like the humans, we sea turtles are shell wearing reptilians that are visually oriented creatures.

We rely on our eye sight to identify other members of the same sea turtle species. We also need our eyes to identify food, and all potential dangers and predators like big fish and sharks.

We sea turtles, for example, are so dependent on our eye sight that when some researchers that blindfolded some of us, we were unable to find our way back into the sea. That's powerful proof!

Research also shows that we sea turtles do not only perceive the colors, but that certain colors like a red, a zesty orange, and a sunny yellow (the really bright colors) seem to be the most appetizing for us sea turtles.

Don't we turtles love to always think about eating?

If we sea turtles really see an object in one of those bright colored shades, we display an "investigative behavior," which suggests that we are checking out what is going on because we'd like to see if we want to eat the red, zesty orange, and sunny yellow colored stuff that we can see!

Aren't we truly weird and amazing creatures at the same time?

For some more weird stuff that you can learn about us, please refer to chapter: "Some Revelations, Truths & Other Curious Stuff About Sea Turtles"

Some Revelations, Truths & Other Curious Stuff About Sea Turtles

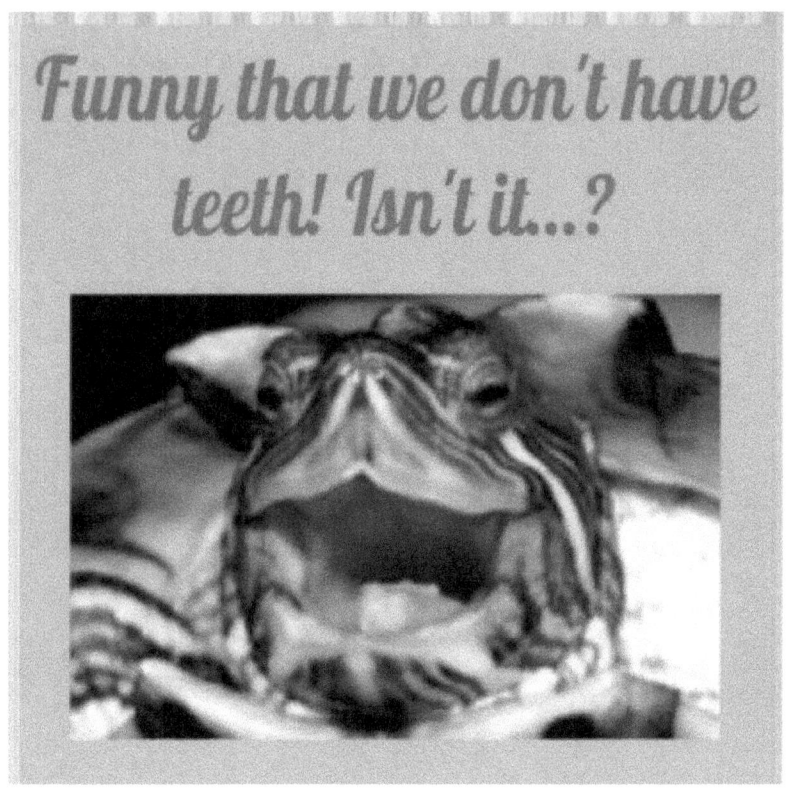

Here are some other really cool and interesting facts about us sea turtles…

1. We sea turtles are like nomads. We can migrate and travel around 1,300 miles per day.

2. We sea turtles carry our shell (our home) on our back and it is tough as a rock. It will never break when we are diving into the ocean.

3. Leatherback Sea turtles can dive more than 300 meters deep.

4. We sea turtles can stay submerged underwater for as long as 5 hours. This is crazy because this activity slows down our heart rate to conserve oxygen.

5. Did you notice that on our shell there are strange markings? From where do these markings come from? Well, a lost culture once believed that they could tell when the end of the world is going to happen just by reading the markings of our shells! How strange is this?

6. In the world's oceans, flatback turtles may spend hours at the surface floating around. Apparently they are asleep or basking in the sun. Frequently, seabirds appear and perch on the backs of the flatback turtles. Can you imagine such a peaceful image? I would say cute, peaceful and beautiful!

7. Olive Ridley turtles have been observed basking on beaches, and it is not unusual to see thousands of Olive Ridleys floating in front of the nesting beaches. Are you inspired by us turtles yet and aren't we a source for creative inspiration?

8. Leatherback turtles tend to dive in a cycle that follows the daily rising and sinking of the dense layer of plankton and jellyfish.

9. We turtles do not have any teeth or whatsoever! Our jaws, however, have modified "beaks" suited to our particular diet.

10. We do not have visible ears neither. We have eardrums that are covered by skin.

11. We sea turtles do hear at low frequencies.

12. As you were able to see in the Mating chapter, we turtles are excellent smellers. Our sense of smell is fabulous.

13. We sea turtles have good vision under water, but we are near-sighted when we are on land.

14. I know we sea turtles are weird so it should not come to you as a surprise that we sea turtles can sleep on the surface of the water and even on the bottom of it. We are haning out and napping under ledges and rocks.

...and last but not least sleeping is one of our favorite past times! Can't you tell?

15. Typically we sea turtles are solitary animals and we do not socialize. We love spending most of our time resting and feeding.

16. Did you know that the Indian Mythology talks about us Sea Turtles?

Did you know that the Indian mythology states that the survival of us sea turtles insures the survival of the globe and the entire world? Didn't I tell you about our secret stuff and our weird behaviors before? Yes, we sea turtles have come a long way since 110 million years and until today. Surviving is what we do best and the Indian mythology gets us.

The Indian mythology has the most beautiful saying about us turtles and it goes like this: "The earth rests on the back of three elephants. These elephants in turn stand on the shell of a giant sea turtle which swims in an infinite sea."

Isn't this mystic saying beautiful? It is my favorite quote from the Indian mythology and I hope this source provides you with some inspiration moments and food for thought, too!

This Indian mythology also believes that the world will end the moment we sea turtles are going to disappear. We can not let our extinction happen because this might end life on earth!

I hope this visual reflection really touches your heart and gives you lots of inspirational thoughts.

We sea turtles are much older and much wiser than the human beings so please do take our species seriously because our existence and co-existance is as important as any other life that needs to be protected and taken care of on this earth. Life on earth does exist because animals, plants, human beings, nature, and a whole array of other things can live together in peace and in co-existance together.

All human beings from all countries of the world need to create a collective consciousness for our cause and we must all be aware of the fact that we sea turtles depend on you human beings and you human beings depend on us sea turtles.

To learn more about how you can help and support us and to make sure that our extinction will never happen, please also read the upcoming chapters where you will learn more about the dangers that we are already facing today and how you can help us.

There are many solutions out there, but everyone must take an initiative.

You can start by becoming aware of our endangered species and by sharing this information with your friends, family, and friends.

Make sure to learn as much as you can about animals like us and other animals, nature, the earth, and many other issues that all concern our life here on earth and our existence and survival.

We need to co-exist together in order to survive and once we have figured out how to care for each other and how to protect each other, we are on the right path!

Make sure to go to the upcoming chapters and the resources chapter to find our more about how we can learn how to co-exist together in harmony and in peace.

Can Sea Turtles Be Kept As Pet?

By now you have gone through a lot of information about us sea turtles and this is the point where you might ask yourself if you would like to keep a turtle as a pet for yourself!

Here are the most critical questions that you should go through before you engage in such a project.

The first step in owning a pet turtle is about understanding the great responsibilities that you as a turtle pet owner have to go through. Taking care of a turtle can be stressful if you do not know from the beginning of what you are getting yourself into.

You have to take care of the turtle on a daily basis and you must be clear on these responsibilities before buying a pet turtle.

Turtles do need a great deal of care. It is legal to own or buy turtles fewer than 4 inches in length, but it is illegal to commercially sell them.

Depending on which type of turtle you prefer, there are different things to know for each breed.

The red ear slider turtle, for example, needs a tank, a heater, a basking light, a UVB light, a filter, a basking area, a thermometer, and of course water.

The tank itself must be a minimum of 20 gallons in size and the bigger the better.

Make sure to check out the basic needs of the specific breed of turtle you want to keep first and inform yourself about every angle that you need to be aware of.

Once you are aware of what a turtle needs and its basic needs, make sure to write them down which makes this whole process more real and feasible.

Also think about your responsibilities as a turtle owner like what are you going to do with the turtle when you leave for the weekend or for a long vacation.

Make sure to discuss your project with your parents first and look at the financial aspect as well. You can make a list of things that you need to buy one time and a list of things that you need to buy on a weekly or daily basis like food for the turtle. If you can not finance the basic needs of a turtle, it makes no sense to keep a pet because it will not be a happy pet without the necessary care.

If you do not have enough money to buy proper food, your turtle will not be able to develop into a healthy turtle because it lacks a proper nutrition.

In this case you might find a way how to earn some of your own money to make sure you can provide everything that a turtle needs or you can go to the zoo and admire the beauty of us turtles in an environment that has the funds to care for us turtles so that we can develop from hatchlings and develop into some beautiful and self-sustainable creatures.

At the zoo everyone has the chance to admire us beautiful creatures. The zoo provides a great opportunity for everyone who loves animals and who can not keep his or her favorite animal at home.

Guess what!

There are even stranger and weirder animals than us turtles that you can visit at the zoo!

Make sure to come up with a wise decision if you can or can not keep a pet turtle and don't be sad if you can't because there are so many other opportunities for you that you can take into consideration to discover more about us, to help, and to support us.

One thing is for sure we do not love to be kept in a tiny space with no food and no room for development. In general, we do not like to be kept in a caged zoo neither because who likes to be kept and taken under surveillance all day long?

Living at the zoo, however, is still better than in a tiny tank where there is no space at all.

Living in our natural habitat and in the oceans of the world is where we are most happy and develp best. There are many risks that we face there and it is a tough fight for us. Only the strongest survive out there because out in the nature by ourselves we have to face many obstacles and remember only 1 hatchling out of 100 hatchlings is going to make it into adulthood.

This is a very creepy number, but having to imagine that one of us has to live in a cage that provides no space at all and without the proper food is an even creepier thought.

This is the reason why you really should make sure to come up with a wise decision that is in favor of us sea turtles and hopefully you will appreciate us for who we are when you are making your decision.

Giving us the proper treatment is the basis for a co-existence between human being and us sea turtles.

Before you go ahead with any turtle pet project, please make sure you consider every aspect and come to a fair judgement.

We need proper treatment and food on a daily basis. Sometimes we might get sick and we need medical care.

Thanks for considering every aspect about us before taking your final decision so that we can develop into a beautiful and happy turtle...

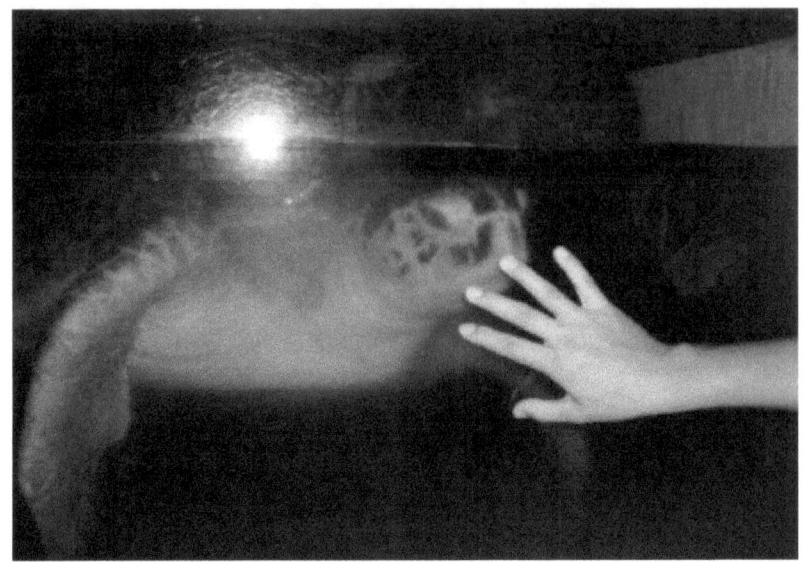

Is The Future Of Sea Turtles In Danger?

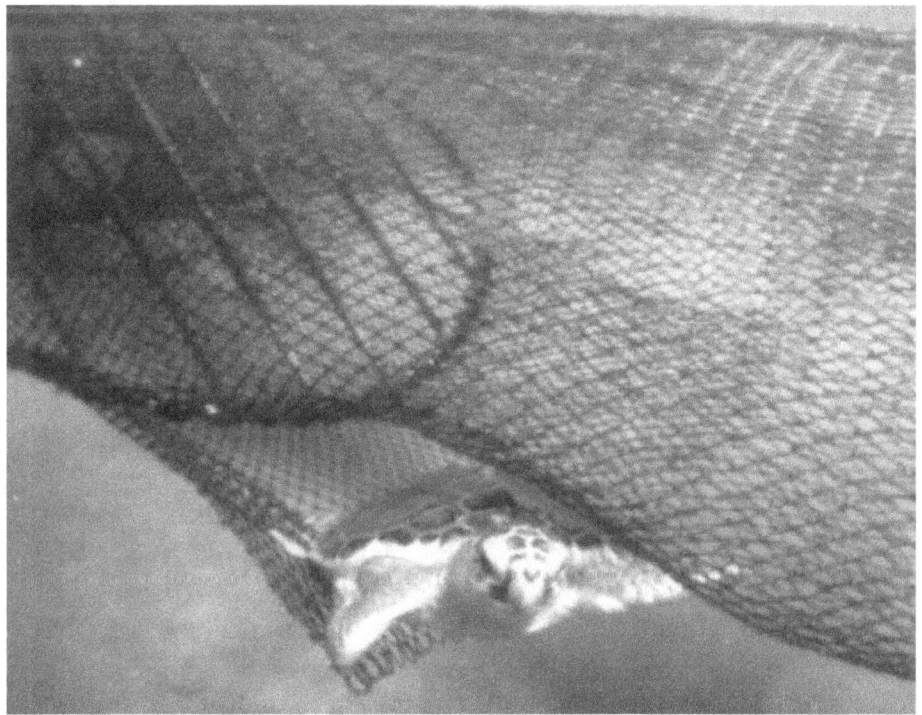

Loggerhead Sea Turtle escaping from a net via TED device

Now that you hopefully can appreciate us and our various species that go from the Leatherbacks to the Loggerheads, you might be interested in some more serious stuff that concerns our future and your future at the same time because we all live on the same planet and we need to make sure that we support each other!

Did you know that seven species of sea turtles are threatened or endangered at the hand of humans?

Yes, it is true and we are very sad about it because we as sea turtles have come such a long way.

Sadly, the fact is that we sea turtles face many dangers as we travel the earth's oceans. These are artificial dangers created by human greed and power.

We have been known to survive and adapt throughout evolution and we are creatures that are well-adapted to nature and the oceans, but we are not able to adapt to artificial human activities that harm us.

Did you know that today only 7 of our species do exist world wide? All of our 7 sea turtle species are listed as "endangered" or "threatened" under the Endangered Species Act.

In nature, we sea turtles face a constant host of life and death obstacles to our daily survival.

Predators such as raccoons, crabs and ants raid the eggs of our female sea turtles.

These enemies raid the nests while the hatchlings are still in there.

Once the babies emerge, these hatchlings provide bite-sized meals for birds who are looking for prey. There are other predators like crabs that are waiting for the hatchlings to arrive in the sea.

Once our hatchlings have passed the most critical age and after reaching adulthood, we sea turtles are relatively immune to predation, except for the occasional shark attacks.

We sea turtles are not immune to these powerful predatators because they are the true killers of the ocean and we are pretty afraid of them.

Only one hatchling in a thousand hatchlings is going to make it to adulthood. Once a sea turtle has reached adulthood, it can live to be over 100 years old.

These natural threats like sharks and other predators, however, are not the real reasons we sea turtle have plummeted toward extinction.

To understand what really threatens the survival of our population, you must look at the actions of humans and what humans do to our beautiful natural habitats.

For example, these harmful human actions include artificial lightning that discourages our female sea turtles from nesting, illegal sea turtle shell trade, commercial fishing, as well as harvesting for consumption, etc.

Our hatchlings, however, are the weakest ones and only 1 in 100 is making it to adulthood.

Our youngest do face many natural predators like dogs, raccoons, and ghost crabs.

Our hatchlings on the beaches are more than easy targets for animal predators.

In the ocean our little ones face larger fishes.

Putting everything into perspective, humans are still our biggest threat and they can really hurt us by interfering with every stage of our life cycle.

I am talking about development at beachfronts, beach nourishment projects, artificial lighting, and driving on beaches, boating, dredging, and fishing

which can all impact the nesting activities of our female sea turtles.

These human activities migh in some cases even prevent our female sea turtles from nesting altogether which is against mother nature's law.

Did you know that sea turtles can even drown when they are entangled in floating trash and garbage?

Sometimes this interaction between us sea turtles and humans might be unintentional, but it is true that the increased human presence in coastal areas may harm, hurt, and even kill us!

Just be aware of the fact that the decisions that you as humans make about playing and living on the coast are extremely critical for our survival!

What can humans do to protect us?

They can put up restrictions on beachfront development, restrictions on artificial lighting, restrictions for beachfront driving, and human beings can also use turtle excluder devices. Today turtle excluder devices are already required by all offshore shrimping boat activities that operate in US waters and from North Carolina to the shores of Texas.

One positive thing that has evolved and that is in place to protect our rights is the fact that some human beings like you showed initiative for our cause and some of you have come up with a law that protects us from international sea turtle trade.

The CITES (short for The Convention on International Trade in Endangered Species Of Wild Fauna and Flora) interdicts the trade of us sea turtles and the CITES bans such activities worldwide.

We are peaceful and non harmful animals and we add natural beauty to the earth and the oceans. We even love to swim with humans when we are very close to the shore.

There is one difference though. We do not kill humans, but humans unintentionally or intentionally might harm and kill us!

Once we have reached adulthood and luckily for those who make it, we won't be a pray so easily.

We are smart, too, you know because otherwise we would not have been able to survive for millions of years until today.

Please refer to the chapter "Please Help Us" where you can see how your initiative might save our species...

Please Help Us

We sea turtles do live a longer lifespan if we live in a protected environment like a zoo. Did you know that we can reach the age of a 100 years?

We are a very friendly species if we are kept in zoos because nobody can attack us and we love to live a peaceful life.

However, if we sea turtles live in the wild, like any other animal, we do fear humans.

Today, more and more of us sea turtles are captivated in zoos around the globe and we are taken care of via some other protection programs by humans who show initiative for our case.

It is very sad that we need such protection programs as opposed to being able to survive ourselves in the wild nature like the rules of mother nature are suggesting it.

However, we are not capable to follow mother nature's law because of some ignorant human beings who harm and kill us and we are therefore very thankful for these protected places that have been created for us and our survival.

Some humans do a lot to help us and to make sure that we sea turtles are well taken care of and that we are protected.

Thanks to those people who are actively helping us through their initiatives.

On the other side, there are other humans who can truly be a serious threat to us sea turtles.

We fear humans who do not respect our freedom and rights. We fear the people who keep hunting us for our beautiful shells. We fear the people who hunt us down for their own benefits and profit.

Because there are humans who hunt us down and who sell us to others, we are now considered an endangered species.

The best way to help us sea turtles is by not buying any such products that are made from our shells.

Conservation efforts and breeding programs are in place to restore our population to a normal level.

Today there are animal rights and laws in place that makes hunting for our us and destructing our habitats illegal.

Thanks for your engagement and initiative in putting out this message to everyone you know because you can make a huge difference! If everybody will put out the message like you do, our terrible endangered condition that we live in today might change for the better tomorrow!

We love peace, we are peaceful animals and we enjoy our happiness!

If you love us sea turtles, too, make sure to defend us against these animal haters who do not seem to care about us and who hunt us down for their own benfits and money gains.

Thanks for sharing the message and thanks for being our fan and friend!

...and make sure to put out this message to others because we are an endangered species and we need Your HELP!

Everybody around the planet needs to get this message!

Important Sea Turtle Resources

International Sea Turtle Observation Registry (iSTOR). Have you ever seen a live sea turtle...?
http://www.seaturtle.org/istor
SC Marine Turtle Conservation - Protecting sea turtles for future generations:
http://www.dnr.sc.gov/seaturtle
Sea Turtles - Project Global:
http://bycatch.nicholas.duke.edu/species/seaturtles
Seven Species of Marine Turtles:
http://worldwildlife.org/species/sea-turtle
Turtle Craft Projects for Kids:
http://www.artistshelpingchildren.org/turtles-tortoises-craftsideasactivitieskids.html
Defenders of Wildlife - Sea turtles are one of the Earth's most ancient creatures. The seven species that can be found today have been around for 120 million years, that's even longer than dinos have been around:
http://www.defenders.org/sea-turtles/basic-facts
Sea Turtles for Kids:
http://www.turtles.org/kids.htm
Sea Turtle Conservancy: Sea Turtles, Their Habitats and Threats to Their Survival:
http://www.conserveturtles.org/seaturtleinformation.php
NOAA Fisheries - Office of Protected Resources:
http://www.nmfs.noaa.gov/pr/species/turtles
SeaWorld/Busch Gardens:
http://www.seaworld.org/infobooks/seaturtle/home.html
The Karen Beasley Sea Turtle Rescue and Rehabilitation Center:
http://www.seaturtlehospital.org
Sea Turtle Statistics:
Seaturtle.org[1]

---

1. http://www.seaturtle.org

Interesting Things to See Near Sunset Beach:
http://www.sunsetbeachnc.gov

The Ocean Isle Museum Foundation, Inc. with the Museum of Coastal Carolina and Ingram Planetarium:
http://museumplanetarium.org

Did you love *Seaturtle Discovery Kids: Sea Stories Of Cute Sea Turtles With Funny Pictures, Photos & Memes Of Seaturtles For Children*? Then you should read *Panda Discovery Kids: Jungle Stories of Cute Panda Bears with Funny Pictures, Photos & Memes of Pandas for Children* by Kate Cruso!

Panda Discovery Kids: Jungle Stories Of Cute Panda Bears With Funny Pictures, Photos & Memes Of Pandas For Children... Inside your child learns about things like: * Lovable Pandas * Pandas Hiding Places * Panda Senses * Pandas Communication * Panda Defense Method * Lots More... + Surprise Bonus Story Inside... If you love Pandas, Animals In Nature, Panda Pictures for Kids, Funny Panda Stories, Amazing Panda Facts For Kids, Kids Book Series you will love this curious & intriguing Panda book! Click the happy button above to get started today...

Also by Kate Cruso

Discovery Books For Kids Series
Frogs And Toads Discovery: Frog Picture Book For Kids With Fun Photos & Illustrations
Panda Discovery Kids: Jungle Stories of Cute Panda Bears with Funny Pictures, Photos & Memes of Pandas for Children
Seaturtle Discovery Kids: Sea Stories Of Cute Sea Turtles With Funny Pictures, Photos & Memes Of Seaturtles For Children

Standalone
Snake Discovery Kids: Jungle Stories Of Mysterious & Dangerous Snakes With Funny Pictures, Photos & Memes Of Snakes For Children

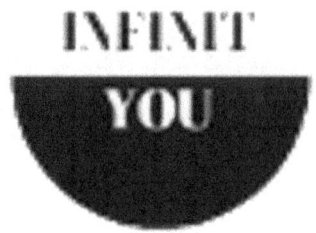

About the Publisher

InfinitYou is a hybrid general interest trade publisher. One of the first of its kind InfinitYou publishes physical books, electronic books, and audiobooks in various genres. Our publications are meant to educate, edify and entertain readers of all walks of life from babies to the elderly.

Home to more than twenty imprints such as Infinit Baby, Infinit Kids, Infinit Girl, Infinit Boy, Infinit Coloring, Infinit Swear Words, Infinit Activities, Infinit Productivity, Infinit Cat, Infinit Dog, Infinit Love, Infinit Family, Infinit Survival, Infinit Health, Infinit Beauty, Infinit Spirituality, Infinit Lifestyle, Infinit Wealth, Infinit Romance, and lots more.

www.ingramcontent.com/pod-product-compliance
Lightning Source LLC
LaVergne TN
LVHW011713060526
838200LV00051B/2892